Bible Principles On How to Lose Weight

Keira O. Ortiz

Introduction

In your quest to achieve and maintain a healthy weight, you'll discover that biblical principles can provide you with valuable insights and guidance. This guide is not just about shedding pounds; it's about finding a balance between physical well-being and spiritual growth.

During our opening session, we'll embark on a journey of self-reflection and introspection. It's crucial to search our hearts and understand our motivations for seeking change. We'll also acknowledge that hope is an essential companion on this journey, and with it, transformation becomes possible.

As we delve deeper into the guide, we'll explore the power of choice and how it aligns with biblical teachings. We are not without agency in our weight management journey, and understanding the freedom to choose empowers us to make healthier decisions.

One of the key aspects we'll focus on is self-control. What does it truly mean to exercise self-control, and how can biblical wisdom guide us in this regard? We'll examine this principle closely, understanding that it plays a fundamental role in achieving and maintaining a healthy weight.

In our tool chest section, we'll equip ourselves with practical strategies. Depriving food of its power over us, addressing emotional eating, and adopting new habits will be discussed. These tools will serve as your companions on this transformative journey.

Finally, in our closing session, we'll engage in a moment of reflection and prayer. Connecting with your faith can provide strength, resolve, and a sense of purpose as you navigate the challenges and triumphs of your weight loss journey.

Remember, this guide is not just about losing weight; it's about discovering a healthier, more balanced you. With faith as your anchor and these biblical principles as your guide, you can embark on this path with confidence and hope. Let's begin this transformative journey together.

Contents

OPENING SESSION

Set the Stage

*B*efore we go even one step further, it's essential to set the stage with this one simple, yet fundamental truth…we act on what we believe.

Luke 6:43-45

[43]No good tree bears bad fruit, nor does a bad tree bear good fruit. [44]Each tree is recognized by its own fruit. People do not pick figs from thornbushes, or grapes from briers. [45]The good man brings good things out of the good stored up in his heart, and the evil man brings evil things out of the evil stored up in his heart. For out of the overflow of his heart his mouth speaks.

Just as each tree is recognized by its own fruit, so our waistlines are determined by the food we eat. So, whatever we believe about food, whether good or bad… right or wrong… is directly reflected in how we act around food. What's more, the assumptions and expectations we internalize over the course of our lives also affect our emotional response when tempted by food.

This explains why traditional dieting never works. We go on diets to lose_____.

Diets only target the weight we see on the outside, while our inside reality stays exactly the same. Consequently, short-term diets seldom ever result in "forever change" because our weight is only a symptom of our behavior.

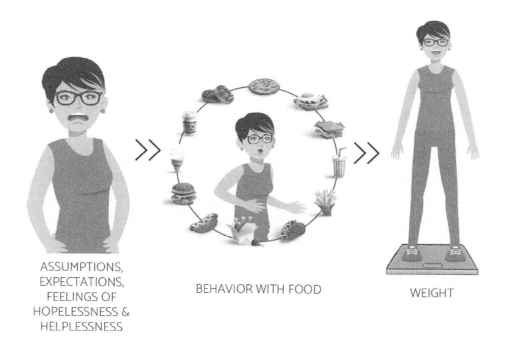

ASSUMPTIONS,
EXPECTATIONS,
FEELINGS OF
HOPELESSNESS &
HELPLESSNESS

BEHAVIOR WITH FOOD

WEIGHT

If we really want to change our weight, then we must change our, _____ because, "out of the overflow of [the] heart [the] mouth speaks."

Video

Refer to the following outline as you watch the video. Make note of anything that stands out to you for further reflection or discussion.

- Our actions with food follow our beliefs

- We feel ashamed and hopeless

- Emotional root to our eating

- 7 goals for this study

 Video Discussion and Bible Study

- In the video Shellie says, "We've all felt it... that frustration of pants that are too tight...of standing there in the closet trying to find clothes that still fit and then finally reverting back to that same go-to outfit you've been wearing everywhere because it's the only thing that still feels comfortable."

- How do you think it will help you to share this journey with others who have felt the way you've felt and who are where you are?

- Are there specific negative emotions that you would like to see God speak truth into during the course of this journey?

Further Discussion

 Set The Stage

1. What is your greatest frustration with your weight?

2. Right now, do you view food more in positive terms or negative terms?

3. Do you believe that God can speak into your weight situation?

Let's look at the goals for our journey.

- See healthy weight management as a journey, rather than a destination

- Regard healthy weight management in terms of daily choices, rather than as an "all or nothing" proposition

- Replace the diet mentality with a long-term mindset

- Become more mindful during every step of the eating process (choices, prep, actually sitting down to eat)

- Learn to bring my struggles with food to God and lay them bare before Him on a regular basis

- Develop a healthy perspective about my weight by accepting the body I have today

- Understand and acknowledge that my worth and value as a child of God is not found in my weight or appearance

TOOL CHEST

Each week, the tool chest will contain your assignments for the following week.

☐ Read the first two chapters of *Find Your Weigh*.

☐ Take your measurements using the guidelines below, to give you a baseline *(these are for your own personal reference).*

☐ Pray and ask God to open your heart to the leading of the Holy Spirit throughout the rest of this journey.

☐ Stock up on some healthy snacks in preparation for Week One. (E.g. roasted nuts, yogurt, lean cheese, fruit, vegetables with yogurt dip).

Take Measurements

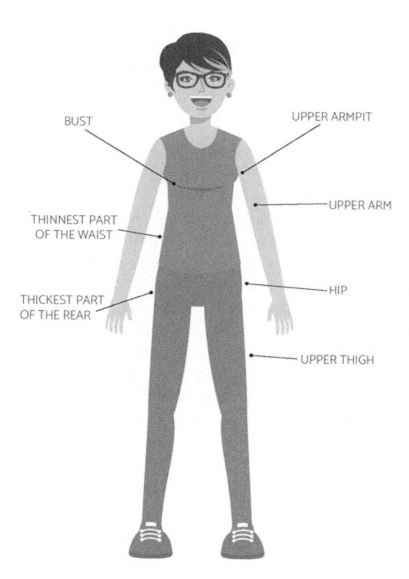

BUST

UPPER ARMPIT

UPPER ARM

THINNEST PART OF THE WAIST

THICKEST PART OF THE REAR

HIP

UPPER THIGH

These measurements are only for your personal reference.

Prayer Time

For many of us, just thinking about tackling the whole food issue can bring up a host of anxious feelings. Be encouraged that there is rest in God's presence. He is greater than our hearts and He knows everything we need to accomplish during the course of this journey.

1 John 3:19-24

[19]This then is how we know that we belong to the truth, and how we set our hearts at rest in his presence [20]whenever our hearts condemn us. For God is greater than our hearts, and he knows everything. [21]Dear friends, if our hearts do not condemn us, we have confidence before God [22]and receive from him anything we ask, because we obey his commands and do what pleases him. [23]And this is his command: to believe in the name of his Son, Jesus Christ, and to love one another as he commanded us. [24]Those who obey his commands live in him, and he in them. And this is how we know that he lives in us: We know it by the Spirit he gave us.

SESSION 1 *Search My Heart*

GOALS REVIEW

- See healthy weight management as a journey, rather than a destination

- Regard healthy weight management in terms of daily choices, rather than as an "all or nothing" proposition

- Replace the diet mentality with a long-term mindset

- Become more mindful during every step of the eating process (choices, prep, actually sitting down to eat)

- Learn to bring my struggles with food to God and lay them bare before Him on a regular basis

- Develop a healthy perspective about my weight by accepting the body I have today

- Understand and acknowledge that my worth and value as a child of God is not found in my weight or appearance

Why do we often associate feelings of shame with the ideas of weight and food?

_____

_____

_____

Video

(Pause Video at 3:43)

Refer to the following outline as you watch the video. Make note of anything that stands out to you for further reflection or discussion.

- Samuel goes out to anoint the future king

- We idolize food

- Ask God to search our hearts

- Journaling

Video Discussion and Bible Study

- Read 1 Samuel 16:6–7.

> [6]When they arrived, Samuel saw Eliab and thought, "Surely the LORD's anointed stands here before the LORD." [7]But the LORD said to Samuel, "Do not consider his appearance or his height, for I have rejected him. The LORD does not look at the things man looks at. Man looks at the outward appearance, but the LORD looks at the heart."

Even Samuel fell into the trap of assuming someone's worth based on his physical appearance. A lot of us are guilty of doing the exact same thing. Do you ever assume people are judging your worth based on your appearance, when in reality, you are likely your own worst critic?

◆ In the video Shellie says, "We've got to start by asking God to search our hearts and open our eyes...because we often don't even realize what motivates our actions when it comes to food. All we know is that we like to eat it. Our experiences, feelings and memories are interwoven into our thinking." How often do you really go to God with your weight frustrations?

◆ Shellie said that journaling was not a normal thing for her to do. How about you? Will it be difficult to discipline yourself to write each day for the next 50 days?

◆ The video quotes Proverbs 29:18 (MSG) to illustrate the value of journaling. "If people can't see what God is doing, they stumble all over themselves; But, when they attend to what he reveals, they are most blessed." Looking back on your weight journey, do you ever feel like you're just stumbling all over yourself?

1 Timothy 4:4-10

4For, everything God created is good and nothing is to be rejected if it is received with thanksgiving, 5because it is consecrated by the word of God and prayer. 6If you point these things out to the brothers, you will be a good minister of Christ Jesus, brought up in the truths of the faith and of the good teaching that you have followed. 7Have nothing to do with godless myths and old wives' tales; rather, train yourself to be godly. [8]For physical training is of some value, but godliness has value for all things, holding promise for both the present life and the life to come. [9]This is a trustworthy saying that deserves full acceptance [10](and for this we labor and strive), that we have put our hope in the living God, who is the Savior of all men, and especially of those who believe.

Verse 4 says, "Everything God created is good and nothing is to be rejected if it is received with thanksgiving."

How might our typical diet attempts be viewed in light of verse 4?

_____

_____

_____

Diets typically put certain food off-limits, which in essence, makes them bad. How might this idea set up an emotional conflict for the believer?

_____

_____

_____

God created food to nourish us, enrich us, and bless us. God's provision of food reveals something about his character.

What do the following verses reveal about God's character?

1. Psalm 146:7, "He upholds the cause of the oppressed and gives food to the hungry. The LORD sets prisoners free."

_____

_____

_____

2. Genesis 9:3 (HCSB), "Every living creature will be food for you; as I gave the green plants, I have given you everything."

_____

_____

_____

3. Psalm 136:25, "He gives food to every creature. His love endures forever."

_____

_____

_____

4. Exodus 16:12 (NET), "I have heard the murmurings of the Israelites. Tell them, 'During the evening you will eat meat, and in the morning you will be satisfied with bread, so that you may know that I am the LORD your God.'"

_____

_____

_____

DISCOVERY QUESTIONS

1. Have you believed or are you currently believing some of the world's lies in regard to your weight or your appearance?

2. Are there times when you have allowed those lies to lead you into dark places?

3. Proverbs 4:23 (NLT) says, "Guard your heart above all else, for it determines the course of your life." Your heart is the storehouse of your beliefs, which ultimately determine your course and behavior with food. What are some practical ways you can improve your thought life during this journey?

Proverbs 29:18 (MSG)
If people can't see what God is doing, they stumble all over themselves; but when they attend to what he reveals, they are most blessed.

Restart Video - Introduce Journaling

Today, participants will start journaling every evening. Review the process of journaling in *Find Your Weigh* (pages 25-28).

TOOL CHEST

☐ Read Chapter 3.

☐ Practice awareness with food. Eat in a seated position without other distractions and chew slowly.

☐ Do not step on a scale for the next 3 weeks.

Prayer Time

Over the next 50 days, you will embark on a journey of self-discovery. Pray that God will reveal himself to you through this process and that He will also reveal your beliefs (your expectations and assumptions) and how they affect your behavior with food.

Pray the words of Psalms 139:23-24 together.

Psalm 139:23-24

[23]Search me, O God, and know my heart; test me and know my anxious thoughts. [24]See if there is any offensive way in me, and lead me in the way everlasting.

On Your Own

In verse 7, Timothy admonishes his hearers to have nothing to do with godless myths and old wives' tales.

As Christians, we may have the "head knowledge" to know that the ways of the world are not supposed to be our ways, but that knowledge does not always translate to our behavior. Luke 6:45 says, "The good man brings good things out of the good stored up in his heart...For out of the overflow of his heart his mouth speaks.

What are some common myths you believe about your appearance and your body?

_____

_____

_____

For a person who struggles with weight, food can be an all-consuming proposition. Either you want it, you are upset that you ate too much of it (again), or you are making a plan to stay away from it.

FYW, p. 6

1 John 1:5-7

[5]This is the message we have heard from him and declare to you: God is light; in him there is no darkness at all. [6]If we claim to have fellowship with him yet walk in the darkness, we lie and do not live by the truth. [7]But

if we walk in the light, as he is in the light, we have fellowship with one another, and the blood of Jesus, his Son, purifies us from all sin.

When we don't feel good about our weight, we can easily allow negative thoughts and self-doubt to invade our lives. In fact, those thoughts can take us to a very dark place; a place God never intends for us to be. This is the time we must take our thoughts captive in obedience to Christ.

1 Corinthians 10:3-5

[3]For though we live in the world, we do not wage war as the world does. [4]The weapons we fight with are not the weapons of the world. On the contrary, they have divine power to demolish strongholds. [3]We demolish arguments and every pretension that sets itself up against the knowledge of God, and we take captive every thought to make it obedient to Christ.

SESSION 2 *We Are Not Without Hope*

GOALS REVIEW

- See healthy weight management as a journey, rather than a destination

- Regard healthy weight management in terms of daily choices, rather than as an "all or nothing" proposition

- Replace the diet mentally with a long-term mindset

- Become more mindful during every step of the eating process (choices, prep, actually sitting down to eat)

- Learn to bring my struggles with food to God and lay them bare before him on a regular basis

- Develop a healthy perspective about my weight by accepting the body I have today

- Understand and acknowledge that my worth and value as a child of God is not found in my weight or appearance

Our struggles with food can convince us that our situation is hopeless.

Romans 7:21-23

[21]So I find this law at work. When I want to do good, evil is right there with me. [22]For in my inner being I delight in God's law; [23]but I see another law at work in the members of my body, waging war against the law of

my mind and making me a prisoner of the law of sin at work within my members.

You've been journaling for a week now and likely, this verse has been playing out in your thinking. How has your body been fighting against your mind this week?

_____

_____

_____

Video

Refer to the following outline as you watch the video. Make note of anything that stands out to you for further reflection or discussion.

- Learned helplessness

- The children of Israel at the brink of possessing the land

- Just because you haven't seen it

Video Discussion and Bible Study

- If we're honest with ourselves, most of us would say we feel or have felt completely helpless when it comes to the temptation of food. Why is this? What makes us so vulnerable?

◆ Read Numbers 13:31-33

> [31]But the men who had gone up with him said, "We
> can't attack those people; they are stronger than we
> are." [32]And they spread among the Israelites a bad
> report about the land they had explored. They said,
> "The land we explored devours those living in it. All the
> people we saw there are of great size. "We saw the
> Nephilim there (the descendants of Anak come from
> the Nephilim). We seemed like grasshoppers in our
> own eyes, and we looked the same to them."

Shellie explains that all twelve Israelites who went to scout out
the land of Canaan shared the same experience of bondage
and that they had been conditioned to feel helpless. Can you
think of past experiences or family/ cultural values that may
have conditioned you to react to food in a certain way?

◆ In the video, Shellie says, "He's given us the Holy Spirit...the
'spirit of Him who raised Jesus from the dead.' And He wants you
to realize to really internalize that amazing reality...that very same
spirit dwells in you!" How might a true realization of this fact help
propel you forward in your journey from this day forward?

————————————

Here are some common scenarios where we often feel helpless
to resist overeating. These situations are uncontrollable and they
wage war against "the law of our minds" and our best intentions...
until we eventually train ourselves to think we are powerless to
resist.

~ Special occasions

- ~ Holiday observances

- ~ Vacations

- ~ Long periods at home

- ~ Unplanned occasions when food is offered

List some features of these situations that often lead to overeating.

_____

_____

_____

Romans 8:1-2, 5-7, 9, 11

[1]Therefore, there is now no condemnation for those who are in Christ Jesus. [2]because through Christ Jesus the law of the Spirit of life set me free from the law of sin and death...

[5]Those who live according to the sinful nature have their minds set on what the flesh desires; but those who live in accordance with the Spirit have their minds set on what the Spirit desires. [6]The mind of sinful man is death, but the mind controlled by the Spirit is life and peace; [7]the sinful mind is hostile to God. It does not submit to God's law, nor can it do so...

[9]You, however, are controlled not by the sinful nature but by the Spirit, if the Spirit of God lives in you. And if anyone does not have the Spirit of Christ, he does not

belong to Christ...[11]And if the Spirit of him who raised Jesus from the dead is living in you, he who raised Christ from the dead will also give life to your mortal bodies through his Spirit, who lives in you.

As believers, we have the "Spirit of him who raised Jesus from the dead" living in us. Look back at the passage above. *What can we expect the Holy Spirit to do in our lives?*

1. In verse 2, "Through Christ Jesus the law of the Spirit of life _____from the law of sin and death."

2. In verse 5, "Those who live in accordance with the Spirit have _____on what the Spirit desires."

3. In verse 6, "The mind controlled by the Spirit is _____and_____."

4. In verse 11 "He who raised Christ from the dead will also

_____ _____ _____ _____ _____

_____through his Spirit, who lives in you."

Find Your Weigh (p. 61-63) offers five practical steps for resisting the mindset of learned helplessness in these situations.

1. _____

2. _____

3. _____

4. _____

5. _____

How might Romans 8:5 be applied to the concept of moderation with food?

_____

_____

_____

DISCOVERY QUESTIONS

1. Let's reflect on the past week. Mindless eating often happens when we are unprepared. What time of day were you most vulnerable to snacking?

2. What practical things can you do to be more mindful during your most vulnerable moments of the day?

3. Our words have meaning and value (Luke 6:45, "The good man brings good things out of the good stored up in his heart...For out of the overflow of his heart his mouth speaks." How might refusing to use the word "diet" help to reinforce a long-term mindset with food?

   If there is time remaining, group members can share their impressions of the first week.

TOOL CHEST

☐ Read Chapter 4.

☐ Beware of falling into the familiar "diet" mentality in order to get quick results.

☐ Physical activity is extremely important. Determine to spend at least 20 minutes a day (or a combined total of 140 minutes/week) doing some type of physical activity.

☐ Planning ahead makes it much easier to make good food choices. Sit down and think through your menu for the week. Make sure to consider your snacks as well...portion out snacks into individual portions.

Prayer Time

Jesus' act of dying on the cross brought an end to death from sin, every sin that separates us from His perfect plan for our lives. Every time we are confronted with our sinful tendencies, we are told to pick up our cross and follow Him afresh and anew.

Matthew 16:24

24Then Jesus said to his disciples, "If anyone would come after me, he must deny himself and take up his cross and follow me."

But God doesn't leave us there to fight this daily battle alone. Instead, He promises to develop our perseverance as we flex our faith muscles. He also promises to give us wisdom where we lack it.

James 1:2-5

2Consider it pure joy, my brothers, whenever you face trials of many kinds, 3because you know that the testing of your faith develops perseverance. [4]Perseverance must finish its work so that you may be mature and complete, not lacking anything. [5]If any of you lacks wisdom, he should ask God, who gives generously to all without finding fault, and it will be given to him.

Let's pray God's Word over this next week of journaling and seeking Him.

God, I consider it pure joy whenever I face trials this week in my journey to overcome my struggles with food, because I know that the testing of my faith develops perseverance. Perseverance must finish its work so that I may be mature and complete, not lacking anything. Since I lack wisdom, I ask you, God, who generously gives wisdom to all without finding fault, and I trust that it will be given to me. Amen.

On Your Own

The idea of learned helplessness is a psychological term that refers to a person's unshakable mindset that she has no control over a particular situation.

FYW, p. 58

This feeling of helplessness and hopelessness is something many of us can relate to in terms of our journey with food. Often, our mental blocks with food have been constructed, brick by brick, from past failures to control our appetites, especially when we find ourselves in tempting situations.

With other objects of addiction, like alcohol or drugs, believers can choose to isolate themselves from all tempting situations. However, we cannot extricate food from our lives, nor can we control the numerous environments where food is eaten.

Romans 8:6 *assures you,*
[6]The mind of sinful man is death, but the mind controlled by the Spirit is life and peace...

What measures can you implement from this day forward to allow the Spirit to consistently speak life and peace into your mind?

_____

_____

_____

What actions do you need to stop or short-circuit that you know are keeping your mind from submitting to the Spirit's control?

_____

_____

_____

In regard to cravings, *FYW* (p.62) suggests, "...by choosing to deprive yourself of a particular food, you attach a negative feeling or emotion to that food. Therefore, to seek balance, your mind will obsess over that food item in an effort to right the wrong and make everything OK again."

Do you agree or disagree with this suggestion?

_____

_____

_____

NOTE: We are not all the same. While some might agree with this statement, others may find that totally abstaining from particular foods better suits their personalities.

How can Romans 8:2 be applied to the person who allows themselves to have a few bites or the person who thinks it's best to totally abstain from eating a particular food?

_____

_____

_____

SESSION 3 *We Have Freedom to Choose*

GOALS REVIEW

- See healthy weight management as a journey, rather than a destination

- Regard healthy weight management in terms of daily choices, rather than as an "all or nothing" proposition

- Replace the diet mentally with a long-term mindset

- Become more mindful during every step of the eating process (choices, prep, actually sitting down to eat)

- Learn to bring my struggles with food to God and lay them bare before him on a regular basis

- Develop a healthy perspective about my weight by accepting the body I have today

- Understand and acknowledge that my worth and value as a child of God is not found in my weight or appearance

We seldom associate the concept of freedom with making wise and thoughtful food choices. In fact, if anything, successful weight management brings just the opposite picture to mind. Usually, we associate strict rules, discipline, and boundaries with making "good" decisions with food.

The conventional take on weight control relies heavily on rules and lists of foods to eat and foods to stay away from. Consequently, when you fail to follow the rules, you feel defeated.

What are some dieting "rules" you have followed in the past?

_____

Video

| Refer to the following outline as you watch the video. Make note of anything that stands out to you for further reflection or discussion. |

◆ Comfortable with a certain perspective

◆ Paul lived with a constant hardship

◆ Life with Christ is a life of decision, freedom to choose

◆ Woman with the issue of blood

Video Discussion and Bible Study

◆ The video raises a common problem. We often expect to fail. Have you lost weight in the past, but deep inside, you expected to gain the weight back?

◆ In the video, Shellie says, "What if we could stop looking at our weight as a list of rules...do this and don't do that...you can eat this, but you can't eat that...but instead, we looked at it...the good, bad and the ugly...the successes and the failures as opportunities to glorify God...opportunities to entrust our weaknesses to Him, so that His power might be displayed."

How might you reframe your weight struggle as a catalyst to revealing God's daily grace in your life?

Read Mark 5:27-29

[27]When she heard about Jesus, she came up behind him the crowd and touched his cloak, [28]because she thought, "If I just touch his clothes, I will be healed."

[29]Immediately her bleeding stopped and she felt in her body that she was freed from her suffering.

◆ Do you relate to the woman with the issue of blood? Have you searched for other solutions to your weight struggle? Are you at the point that you are desperate enough to reach out to Jesus as your only viable solution?

In week two, we learned that Christ's work on the cross set us free from the law of sin and death (Romans 8:2). Your freedom has been secured once and for all, but you have to stand firm upon that freedom. That point has already been established...now you have a decision to make. Will you view your food choices as opportunities to exercise your God-given freedom or as the burden you must bear? It's all about perspective.

When Goliath came against the Israelites, the soldiers all thought, "He's so big we can never kill him." But David looked at the same giant and thought, "He's so big, I can't miss."
Willy Smith
www.christianquotes.com

1 Corinthians 10:23-26

[23]Everything is permissible"—but not everything is beneficial. "Everything is permissible"—but not everything is constructive. [24]Nobody should seek his own good, but the good of others. [25]Eat anything sold in the meat market without raising questions of conscience, [26]for, "The earth is the Lord's and everything in it."

All food is literally on the table for you to eat, so you are free to dive in. But, look at verse 23. Just because everything is permissible does not mean that eating anything and everything you want is _____or_____.

So, how do we determine what's beneficial and constructive? Jesus gave us the perfect criteria for making our food choices. When the Pharisees asked him what the greatest commandment in the Law was, he answered,

Matthew 22:37-39

[37]"'Love the Lord your God with all your heart and with all your soul and with all your mind.' [38]This is the first and greatest commandment. [39]And the second is like it: 'Love your neighbor as yourself.'"

According to the verse above, what two commandments or criteria should we follow when choosing what to eat in any given situation?

1. _____ _____ _____
_____ _____ with all your heart and with all your soul and with all your mind.

2. _____ _____ _____ as
yourself.

Let's continue reading in 1 Corinthians 10:27-31 to see what this looks like in actual practice.

> [27]If some unbeliever invites you to a meal and you want to go, eat whatever is put before you without raising questions of conscience. [28]But if anyone says to you, "This has been offered in sacrifice," then do not eat it, both for the sake of the man who told you and for conscience' sake—[29]the other man's conscience, I mean not yours. For why should my freedom be judged by another's conscience? [30]If I take part in the meal with thankfulness, why am I denounced because of something I thank God for? [31]So whether you eat or drink or whatever you do, do it all for the glory of God.

The Corinthian Christians held conflicting opinions on what to do about eating food sacrificed to idols. Although we don't typically face this situation in our everyday lives, we regularly find ourselves in circumstances where we are not in control of the types of foods we are offered. However, Paul goes right back to Jesus' two commandments/criteria when addressing this issue: the goal is to honor God and love your neighbor.

Let's say you are invited to eat at a friend's house and you know that you will be served foods that you don't typically eat.

What will you do according to verse 27?

_____

_____

_____

And, why will you do it according to verse 31?

_____

_____

_____

Right there, Paul provided us with the perfect example of how to exercise the entertainment vs. fuel principle. Let's look at the Entertainment vs. Fuel Mental Checklist (*FYW*, p. 71-73).

1. _____

2. _____

3. _____

4. _____

5. _____

6. _____

DISCOVERY QUESTIONS

1. Have you been in a situation where you exercised the entertainment model successfully? Did you find it difficult to enjoy the foods on hand and still stay mindful about your choices or did you feel more confident and prepared?

2. What ways have you learned to modify the foods you keep on hand to provide more healthier options?

3. Are you developing a growing satisfaction with your "new normal" or do you feel consistently unsatisfied?

TOOL CHEST

☐ Read Chapter 5.

☐ Begin implementing the five steps to overcome the mental block of learned helplessness, making a conscious effort to visually cut portion sizes.

☐ You should be starting to recognize typical go-to behaviors you have with food. Take time to list those behaviors when you recognize them.

Prayer Time

Galatians 5:1
It is for freedom that Christ has set us free. Stand firm, then, and do not let yourselves be burdened again by a yoke of slavery.

Let's pray together:

Christ, you set me free to experience freedom in you. Change my perspective and help me to learn to make my food choices in light of that freedom. Keep me mindful of times when I am tempted to fall into my old patterns. Help me to stand firm.

 On Your Own

The teachings of the New Testament consistently call us to evaluate our hearts and our motives, and then, to act accordingly.

Colossians 2:20-23
[20]Since you died with Christ to the basic principles of this world, why, as though you still belonged to it, do you submit to its rules: [21]"Do not handle! Do not taste! Do not touch!"? [22]These are all destined to perish with us, because they are based on human commands and teachings. [23]Such regulations indeed have an appearance of wisdom, with their self-imposed worship, their false humility and their harsh treatment of the

body, but they lack any value in restraining sensual indulgence.

If knowing the right things to eat was the only issue, then no one would have to struggle with their weight.

The end of Colossians 2:23 explains why rules and regulations alone, even though they have the appearance of wisdom (and in many cases are nutritionally sound), are not sufficient for transforming our behavior with food.

They lack _____

_____

Ultimately, our perspective determines how we view life. That's why one person sees the glass as half-full, while the other views it as half-empty; why one person sees the job as half-done when another only moans about how much they still have to do. What if we could realign our perspective to see our food choices as an exercise in freedom, rather than as required adherence to a list of rules, shoulds and should-not's?

Galatians 5:1
It is for freedom that Christ has set us free. Stand firm, then, and do not let yourselves be burdened again by a yoke of slavery.

What did Christ set us free for?

_____

_____

_____

SESSION 4 *What Does Self-Control Look Like?*

GOALS REVIEW

◆ See healthy weight management as a journey, rather than a destination

◆ Regard healthy weight management in terms of daily choices, rather than as an "all or nothing" proposition

◆ Replace the diet mentally with a long-term mindset

◆ Become more mindful during every step of the eating process (choices, prep, actually sitting down to eat)

◆ Learn to bring my struggles with food to God and lay them bare before him on a regular basis

◆ Develop a healthy perspective about my weight by accepting the body I have today

◆ Understand and acknowledge that my worth and value as a child of God is not found in my weight or appearance

Typically, the struggle with maintaining weight is attributed to a lack of willpower. In fact, our repeated inability to exercise this often elusive skill set is viewed as a character flaw or personal failure. This sense that we've missed the mark is often further magnified in our thinking, because we see our weight as an outward indication or advertisement of our internal struggle.

Why do you think your willpower has let you down in the past?

_____

_____

_____

Video

◆ Self-control is mentioned last

◆ Christian often avoid talking about food or weight

◆ Your weight is not who you are

◆ We fail to recognize our food struggle as a spiritual weakness

◆ Mid-way assessment

Video Discussion and Bible Study

◆ In the video Shellie says, "We often use the word willpower in reference to our ability to withstand temptation. But, I find this term lacks an essential element...the life-giving, empowering work of the Holy Spirit."

How often have you blamed your food struggle on a lack of willpower?

- Are you proactive in approaching God with your food struggles or do you often wait until you are frustrated and discouraged before you go to Him? Why do we seldom go to God with this issue?

- We have a tendency to compartmentalize our food struggle. How could regarding your food struggle in spiritual terms, rather than only as a physical issue, help you to keep in step with the Spirit?

Galatians 5:22-25

[22]But the fruit of the Spirit is love, joy, peace, patience, kindness, goodness, faithfulness, [23]gentleness and self-control. Against such things there is no law. [24]Those who belong to Christ Jesus have crucified the sinful nature with its passions and desires. [25]Since we live by the Spirit, let us keep in step with the Spirit.

Most likely, you can recall times when lack of self-control over food caused you to experience less of the other fruits of the Spirit. Take a moment to consider how your lack of self-control has robbed you of displaying other fruit in your life (Allow participants to share if they want to).

In this weight journey, it's important to continually evaluate your goals. At this point, you have navigated three weeks of self-introspection through journaling and, hopefully, awareness is becoming more automatic. But, you should also keep one thought in the forefront...thinness is not a fruit of the Spirit.

Ultimately, we want our life to reflect the fruits of the Spirit. God is most concerned with our internal transformation, not our external one.

2 Peter 1:5-6 illustrates the type of results we are looking for.

> [5]For this very reason, make every effort to add to your faith goodness, and to goodness, knowledge; [6]and to knowledge, self-control; and to self-control, perseverance, and to perseverance, godliness.

In this weight journey:

Knowledge + Self-control + Perseverance = Godliness

- Knowledge - insight through journaling

- Self-control - increased awareness and purposeful habits

- Perseverance - long-term mindset

- Godliness - in step with God (Galatians 5:25 says, "Since we live by the Spirit, let us keep in step with the Spirit.")

> *Once I got a handle on the truth about food and my relationship and response to it, then I felt free to exercise more self-control.*
>
> **FYW, p. 18**

Tasty food is difficult to resist. When we are faced with it, our self-control muscles are seriously tested. *Find Your Weigh* (p. 97-99) offers three tips for breaking the yummy food cycle.

Let's look at each of these:

1. _____

2. _____

3. _____

DISCOVERY QUESTIONS

1. How is your mental game going (are you still battling with negative self-talk)? Do you still find yourself going back and forth on whether you should eat something that you have determined you shouldn't?

2. Brainstorm on some strategies to stop the negative self-talk cycle.

3. Is godliness and increased self-control your ultimate goal in this process or do you still find yourself motivated mostly by the idea of being thinner? If weight is still your motivating factor, how might shifting your focus help you to be more successful? (Jeremiah 29:11-13, "For I know the plans I have for you, declares the Lord, plans to prosper you and not to harm you, plans to give you hope and a future. Then you will call upon me and come and pray to me, and I will listen to you. You will seek me and find me when you seek me with all your heart.")

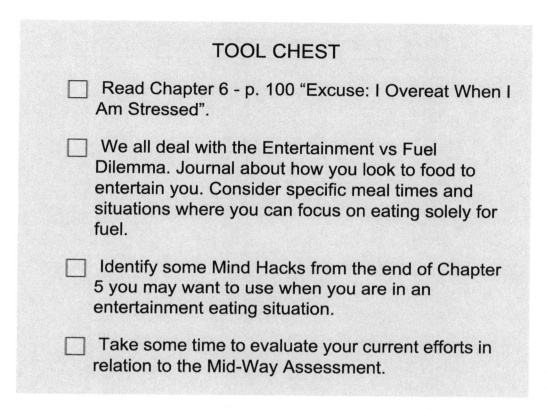

TOOL CHEST

☐ Read Chapter 6 - p. 100 "Excuse: I Overeat When I Am Stressed".

☐ We all deal with the Entertainment vs Fuel Dilemma. Journal about how you look to food to entertain you. Consider specific meal times and situations where you can focus on eating solely for fuel.

☐ Identify some Mind Hacks from the end of Chapter 5 you may want to use when you are in an entertainment eating situation.

☐ Take some time to evaluate your current efforts in relation to the Mid-Way Assessment.

You have just finished the first three weeks of journaling. Likely, some of you stepped on the scale today for the first time since starting your journey. Let's look at the Mid-Way Assessment to consider your progress at the half-way point.

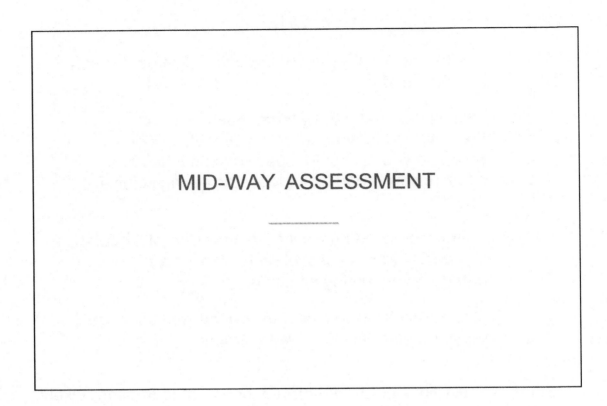

MID-WAY ASSESSMENT

Why did we wait until now to discuss these things?

- The first three weeks you have focused your attention solely on breaking the results/diet mentality.

- You have had three weeks to slowly adjust to eating less food as part of your new normal.

The recommended rate of safe weight loss is 1 to 2 pounds per week.

- Keeps the body from going into starvation mode

- Gives you time to allow your head to catch up with your body (*FYW,* p. 50)

It takes a deficit of 3,500 calories to lose one pound.

- The average woman (age 31-50) burns:

  - 1,800 calories/day

  - 2,000 calories/day (moderately active)

  - 2,200 calories/day (active)

While the skills you are learning will certainly help you maintain your weight from now on, some of you may need to implement further measures to lose weight at this point.

There are 3 ways to do this:

1. Strict adherence to calorie reduction.

2. Add significant exercise to the habits you have started.

3. Mindful calorie reduction plus dedicated attention to increased exercise and movement.*

* This is the most workable option based on the principles we have learned so far.

Consider following the nutrition guidelines of the American Heart Institute. Also, use the Visual Comparison Guide in *FYW*, p. 108.

Daily Servings	
Vegetables	5 servings/day
Fruits	4 servings/day
Fats/oils	3 servings/day
Grains (carbs)	6 servings/day
Dairy	3 servings/day

Weekly Servings	
Poultry, meat, eggs	8 to 9 servings/week
Fish and other seafood	2 to 3 servings/week
Nuts and beans	5 servings/week

Prayer Time

Titus 2:11-12

[11]For the grace of God that brings salvation has appeared to all men. [12]It teaches us to say "No" to ungodliness and worldly passions, and to live self-controlled, upright and godly lives in this present age."

Although our hearts are reconciled to God, our bodies continue to struggle with our earthly desires. Still, we are not without hope because we have a comforter who helps us to say "no" to the draw of food that threatens to rob us of the fruit of self-control in our lives.

Today, let's pray for God's grace and the Spirit's reminder to say "NO" when we are tempted to fall short of our goals and His best.

_____

On Your Own

The dictionary definition of willpower is control exerted to do something or restrain impulses. While successful weight maintenance does require a sustained level of control and restraint, willpower in itself is not adequate. We need the Holy Spirit's consistent help and sustaining empowerment to keep our resolve.

Galatians 5:16-17

¹⁶So I say, live by the Spirit, and you will not gratify the desires of the sinful nature. ¹⁷For the sinful nature desires what is contrary to the Spirit, and the Spirit what is contrary to the sinful nature. They are in conflict with each other, so that you do not do what you want.

When thinking of your weight journey, it's essential to develop a long-term mindset... you are running a marathon, not a sprint. What does the last sentence of verse 17 say about the sinful nature and the Spirit?

_____

_____

_____

> *...There is a struggle between the old nature and the new nature, the remainders of sin and the beginnings of grace, and this Christians must expect will be their exercise as long as they continue in this world.*
>
> (Matthew Henry's Commentary on the Galatians 5:16-17, PC Study Bible Formatted Electronic Database Copyright©2006 by Biblesoft, Inc.)

Because your weakness with food is likely to be ongoing, the modifications you have made to your eating habits over the last three weeks must develop into new life-long habits you can see yourself following next week, next month, and next year.

List some changes you have already made in your eating habits.

    1. _____

    2. _____

    3. _____

Can you envision yourself continuing these habits for the long haul?

_____

_____

_____

SESSION 5 *Deprive Food of Its Power*

GOALS REVIEW

- See healthy weight management as a journey, rather than a destination

- Regard healthy weight management in terms of daily choices, rather than as an "all or nothing" proposition

- Replace the diet mentally with a long-term mindset

- Become more mindful during every step of the eating process (choices, prep, actually sitting down to eat)

- Learn to bring my struggles with food to God and lay them bare before him on a regular basis

- Develop a healthy perspective about my weight by accepting the body I have today

- Understand and acknowledge that my worth and value as a child of God is not found in my weight or appearance

Food raises an all-too-familiar paradox. Initially, you turn to rich foods to make you feel happy and satisfied in the moment, but then, you end up feeling far worse when you are left to deal with the extra weight that cannot be lost in a moment.

It's like locking yourself in a windowless room because it feels cool and cozy only to discover you feel trapped because there is no light coming in from the outside.

Colossians 3:5

Put to death, therefore, whatever belongs to your earthly nature: sexual immorality, impurity, lust, evil desires and greed, which idolatry.

I like how the Amplified Version puts it.

Colossians 3:5 (Amplified Bible)
Put to death and DEPRIVE OF POWER the evil longings of your earthly body [with its sensual, self-centered instincts].

After struggling for years with your weight, it's easy to come to the place where you feel powerless to the lure of food. But through Christ, you can deprive food of its power in and over your life.

What are some ways or situations where we allow food to exert power over our lives?

_____

_____

_____

Video

> *Refer to the following outline as you watch the video. Make note of anything that stands out to you for further reflection or discussion.*

- We love to put things on pedestals

- The children of Israel failed to tear down the high places

- Firefighters fight fire with fire

- Destroy arguments

- Take every thought captive

 Video Discussion and Bible Study

- In the video, Shellie says "We can invest food with so much power, that it becomes our comfort when we are down... or entertainment when we are bored... our confidant when we feel wronged. We can get to the point where food gradually dictates our every move."

  Have you noticed any patterns in the last two weeks of journaling that reveal just how much power you have given up to food?

- Are you beginning to be more mindful about the things you eat?

- Read 2 Corinthians 10:4-6.

  [4]The weapons we fight with are not the weapons of the world. On the contrary, they have divine power to demolish strongholds. [5]We demolish arguments and every pretension that sets itself up against the knowledge of God, and we take captive every thought to make it obedient to Christ. [6]And we will be ready to punish every act of disobedience, once your obedience is complete.

  Have you discovered any arguments or obstacles that need to be destroyed? Are you starting to see how much influence your thoughts have on your food choices?

The idea of putting something to death means you must put up a fight. But frankly, this whole struggle with food may have beaten you down so much in the past that you are convinced that you have no fight left.

But here's the great thing about God. He never tells you to do something without giving you the means to succeed. Paul says that we should put our earthly nature and longings to death. Earlier in verses 2 and 3, Paul reveals the weapons you will need to wage war.

> Colossians 3:2-3
>
> [2]Set your minds on things above, not on earthly things.
>
> [3]For you died, and your life is now hidden with Christ in God.

According to verses 2 and 3, what are the three things you must do (actions) before you can put anything to death or deprive it of its power?

1. _____

2. _____

3. _____

Two of these action words occur immediately when you come to Christ. You die to yourself and you are immediately hidden in Christ.

However, you are told to "set your minds," which requires a present, daily determination. Every day requires a fresh determination to set your minds against tempting situations that threaten to rob you of your power in Christ.

How do you set your mind with food? You have to decide what you will do and how you will act before you find yourself in a tempting situation.

> *You have to short-circuit the "immediate" eat response. The time to come up with alternative activities to eating is before you put any food in your mouth.*
>
> FYW, **p. 94**

Most overeating is mindless eating. We condition ourselves to turn our attention to food whenever our mind is not focused on something else.

Find Your Weigh (p. 90) offers practical steps to stop the "immediate eat" response. Ask yourself:

1. _____

2. _____

3. _____

DISCOVERY QUESTIONS

1. Do you need to develop some new hobbies or clear certain foods from your kitchen? Discuss some practical ways you can take back the power over food in your life.

2. In addition to the steps above, it is also helpful to have something available to think on when your thoughts wander to food. What is your favorite song or Bible verse?

3. Are you beginning to listen to your body for cues to tell you when you are hungry? Have you considered listening to your body, rather than allowing the clock to tell you when you should eat?

TOOL CHEST

☐ Read the rest of Chapter 6 (from page 100) through Chapter 7 to page 116, "Motivation Sapper: Not Drinking Enough Water."

☐ We are often comfortable with our excuses when it comes to eating. Pay attention to the excuses you use to overeat.

☐ Look at the list on page 89, choose two activities to perform at home this week at a time when you are particularly prone to snacking.

Prayer Time

Sing or recite the words of the following song as your closing prayer.

What A Friend We Have In Jesus

What a friend we have in Jesus
All our sins and griefs to bear!
What a privilege to carry
Everything to God in prayer!
Oh what peace we often forfeit
Oh what needless pain we bear
All because we do not carry
Everything to God in prayer

Have we trials and temptations?
Is there trouble anywhere?
We should never be discouraged
Take it to the Lord in prayer
Can we find a friend so faithful
Who will all our sorrows share?
Jesus knows our every weakness
Take it to the Lord in prayer

Are we weak and heavy laden,
Cumbered with a load of care?
Precious Savior, still our refuge
Take it to the Lord in prayer
Do thy friends despise, forsake thee?
Take it to the Lord in prayer!

In his arms he'll take and shield thee
Thou wilt find a solace there

 On Your Own

Social eating and home-alone situations pose a particularly difficult battle.

Have you started constructing your mental battle plan to confront particularly difficult food scenarios?

_____

_____

_____

SESSION 6 *Emotional Eating Does Not Satisfy*

GOALS REVIEW

- See healthy weight management as a journey, rather than a destination

- Regard healthy weight management in terms of daily choices, rather than as an "all or nothing" proposition

- Replace the diet mentally with a long-term mindset

- Become more mindful during every step of the eating process (choices, prep, actually sitting down to eat)

- Learn to bring my struggles with food to God and lay them bare before him on a regular basis

- Develop a healthy perspective about my weight by accepting the body I have today

- Understand and acknowledge that my worth and value as a child of God is not found in my weight or appearance

Life is not always easy and answers seldom come quickly, so it's not surprising that we often turn to food for comfort. While food can momentarily distract us from our worries, it can never satisfy an emotional hurt or longing.

Food can only satisfy physical hunger and even then, it only satisfies for a limited period of time.

Let's test the staying power of food with a simple activity. Place one tasty item in your mouth and time how long you receive flavor satisfaction from it. How long did the flavor/distraction last?

 Video

Refer to the following outline as you watch the video. Make note of anything that stands out to you for further reflection or discussion.

◆ Our memories are strongly linked to food

◆ We rely on food as an escape

◆ Emotional pain comes from a breakdown in our relationships

◆ Life's greatest moments are shared with others

◆ We rely on food to soothe us

 Video Discussion and Bible Study

◆ In the video, Shellie says "We are emotional beings. Many of us have precious memories linked to food...these memories can

evoke warm feelings of joy and contentment...feelings that stand in stark contrast to some of the realities of our daily lives."

- What are some of your favorite food memories?

- How could you reframe your memory to focus more on the people or the experience you shared rather than on the food?

Emotional eating cannot solve your problems, but Jesus can!

> Matthew 11:28-30
> [28]"Come to me, all you who are weary and burdened, and I will give you rest. [29]Take my yoke upon you and learn from me, for I am gentle and humble in heart, and you will find rest for your souls. [30]For my yoke is easy and my burden is light."

Jesus understands what it feels like to be hungry. He also understands how vulnerable and tempted we can be when it comes to food and our appetites, especially when we've been tried or tested.

> Matthew 4:1-4
> [1]Then Jesus was led by the Spirit into the desert to be tempted by the devil. [2]After fasting forty days and forty nights, he was hungry. [3]The tempter came to him and said, "If you are the Son of God, tell these stones to become bread." [4]Jesus answered, "It is written, 'Man does not live on bread alone, but on every word that comes from the mouth of God.'"

In spite of His hunger, Jesus knew that bread was not the answer. Instead of bread, what does Jesus say we need to live?

_____

_____

_____

Emotional eating typically involves two harmful food situations.

1. Eating alone - First question in the Fuel vs. Entertainment Mental Checklist (*FYW* p. 71).

2. Mindless Eating - Remember, we have talked a lot about pre-portioning our food before we eat it.

Find Your Weigh (p. 102-104) offers three tips for breaking the stressed eating cycle. Let's look at each of these.

1. _____

2. _____

3. _____

DISCOVERY QUESTIONS

1. Have you started naturally making a mental plan when you know you will be faced with temptation?

2. Are there still emotional situations that immediately trigger thoughts of food as a way of escape or comfort?

3. How is your mental game going (are you still battling with negative self-talk)? Do you still find yourself going back and forth about whether to eat something that you know you shouldn't?

TOOL CHEST

☐ Read the remainder of Chapter 7 and Chapter 8.

☐ How does your body respond to stress? Does your face get hot or do your hands tremble? Determine your physical trigger response.

☐ Choose a calming action to perform when you feel stressed (*FYW*, p. 104).

Prayer Time

Read the verses below and then offer them to the Lord in prayer.

Prayer of Petition: Psalm 139:23-24

[23]Search me, O God, and know my heart; test me and know my anxious thoughts. [24]See if there is any offensive way in me, and lead me in the way everlasting.

Prayer of Declaration: Psalm 63:5

My soul will be satisfied as with the richest of foods; with singing lips my mouth will praise you.

On Your Own

Stress and emotional eating can easily become a cycle. It's common to hear of people putting on large amounts of weight after a stressful event occurs in their lives.

Thankfully, we have an advocate who can sympathize with our weaknesses because he was "tempted in every way, just as we are."

Hebrews 4:15-16

[15]For we do not have a high priest who is unable to sympathize with our weaknesses, but we have one who

has been tempted in every way, just as we are–yet was without sin. [16]Let us then approach the throne of grace with confidence, so that we may receive mercy and find grace to help us in our time of need.

Jesus understands your emotional struggles. We've already discussed that Jesus knows what it's like to experience physical hunger. Now, let's consider other emotions He encountered when He lived on earth. Read the passage and then write down the emotion Jesus would have felt.

1. Mark 14:37 ~ Then he returned to his disciples and found them sleeping. "Simon," he said to Peter, "are you asleep? Couldn't you keep watch for one hour?"

   _____

   _____

   _____

2. Mark 8:15-19 (ERV) ~ [15]Jesus warned them, "Be careful! Guard against the yeast of the Pharisees and the yeast of Herod." [16]The followers discussed the meaning of this. They said, "He said this because we have no bread." [17]Jesus knew that the followers were talking about this. So he asked them, "Why are you talking about having no bread? Do you still not see or understand? Are you not able to understand? [18]Do you have eyes that can't see? Do you have ears that can't hear? Remember what I did before, when we did not have enough bread? [19]I divided five loaves of bread for 5000 people. Remember how many baskets you filled with pieces of food that were not eaten?"

_____

_____

_____

3. Matthew 26:39 ~ Going a little farther, He fell with his face to the ground and prayed, "My Father, if it is possible, may this cup be taken from me. Yet not as I will, but as you will."

_____

_____

_____

In addition to these emotions, Jesus also had to deal with disappointing His followers who expected Him to establish an earthly kingdom; He carried a huge burden of responsibility on His shoulders and He was known to work very late hours deep into the night.

SESSION 7 *Time to Put on Something New*

GOALS REVIEW

- See healthy weight management as a journey, rather than a destination

- Regard healthy weight management in terms of daily choices, rather than as an "all or nothing" proposition

- Replace the diet mentally with a long-term mindset

- Become more mindful during every step of the eating process (choices, prep, actually sitting down to eat)

- Learn to bring my struggles with food to God and lay them bare before him on a regular basis

- Develop a healthy perspective about my weight by accepting the body I have today

- Understand and acknowledge that my worth and value as a child of God is not found in my weight or appearance

What if I were to send you into a dressing room and ask you to pass all of your old clothes to me as I waited outside, leaving you standing alone in your birthday suit? I'm sure you would be bewildered and unsure of what to do next. Then, what if you were further jolted by the sound of my footsteps receding down the hall... what would you do? Of course, you would yell out to me, "Bring back my clothes or give me something else to wear!"

Ah, and that is exactly where we find ourselves today in this final week of the journey. For six weeks, we have peeled off layer after layer of old thinking and old ways of doing things. Now, it's time to put on something new; otherwise, you risk the likelihood of falling right back into the same old patterns, just like grabbing a favorite sweater on a cold day.

What are some new habits you are already forming?

_____

_____

_____

Video

> *Refer to the following outline as you watch the video. Make note of anything that stands out to you for further reflection or discussion.*

◆ A corrupted battery has no power

◆ We go back to the same habits over and over

◆ Putting on new habits

◆ It's a divine partnership between you and God

 Video Discussion and Bible Study

◆   Jesus healed the lame man at the Pool of Bethesda. Then, when he saw the man again at the temple grounds, he spoke to him.

John 5:14-15

[14]Later Jesus found him at the temple and said to him, "See, you are well again. Stop sinning or something worse may happen to you." [15]The man went away and told the Jews that it was Jesus who had made him well.

Why would Jesus give this warning to the man if he was already healed?

◆   Jesus also refused to cast judgement on the woman caught in the act of adultery.

◆   Read John 8:10-11.

[10]Jesus straightened up and asked her, "Woman, where are they? Has no one condemned you?" [11]"No one, sir," she said. "Then neither do I condemn you," Jesus declared. "Go now and leave your life of sin."

Her accusers were gone and the crisis point had passed. Jesus did not condemn her, but He also did not want her to continue the same patterns. Why?

◆   Do you recognize how your old food habits actually made you more vulnerable to the draw of food?

◆   How might you relate your need to establish new, workable food habits to Jesus' warning to these two people?

Your new thinking about food and your behavior with it and around it must now be translated into action and then perpetually reinforced with new thoughtful habits.

> Ephesians 4:22-28
>
> [22]You were taught, with regard to your former way of life, to put off your old self, which is being corrupted by its deceitful desires; [23]to be made new in the attitude of your minds; [24]and to put on the new self, created to be like God in true righteousness and holiness. [25]Therefore each of you must put off falsehood and speak truthfully to his neighbor, for we are all members of one body. [26]In your anger do not sin": Do not let the sun go down while you are still angry, [27]and do not give the devil a foothold. [28]He who has been stealing must steal no longer, but must work, doing something useful with his own hands, that he may have something to share with those in need.

Verses 22-24 prescribe two equal and opposite actions that you must do in regard to your former way of life in order to be made new in the attitude of your minds.

1. _____ your old self.

2. _____ your new self.

Let's take a closer look at the last verse in this passage.

> [28]He who has been stealing must steal no longer, but must work, doing something useful with his own hands,

that he may have something to share with those in need.

Is a thief who first comes to Christ still a thief?

_____

_____

_____

Well, we could definitely say he has the potential and the resources to no longer be a thief; however, the only way a thief can shed the title for good is to stop stealing.

In other words, the thief must come up with something else to do to make his living instead of stealing...he must put off his old ways and put on new ways to replace them. It's not enough to expect the thief to merely stop stealing, because the stealing served a purpose and met his needs. Instead, he has to come up with alternative, productive ways of living that still meet the same basic needs.

So far, you've uncovered a host of go-to reasons that caused you to give in to the temptation of overindulging your desire for food. Your old behavior with food served a purpose, it:

- ~ entertained you
- ~ soothed you
- ~ gave you instant gratification
- ~ gave you something to do
- ~ allowed you to exercise control
- ~ kept your thoughts occupied
- ~ comforted you

It's easy to deceive ourselves into thinking food can actually solve any of these circumstances in a significant way.

Ephesians 4:22-24
...put off your old self, which is being corrupted by its deceitful desires; [23]to be made new in the attitude of your minds; [24]and to put on the new self, created to be like God in true righteousness and holiness.

We are easily deceived because our old self is_____by its deceitful desires.

Like an old battery, an object that is corrupted is of no use and provides no practical power.

However, putting on a new self by way of new habits helps you to approach food realistically for what it can and cannot do for you. It also provides the structure and discipline to meet your needs in a productive way.

There is one habit that should be considered a one-size-fits-all habit...if you find yourself in a dark place, STEP BACK INTO THE LIGHT!

1 John 1:5-9
[5]This is the message we have heard from him and declare to you: God is light; in him there is no darkness at all. [6]If we claim to have fellowship with him yet walk in the darkness, we lie and do not live by the truth. [7]But if we walk in the light, as he is in the light, we have fellowship with one another, and the blood of Jesus, his Son, purifies us from all sin. [8]If we claim to be without sin, we deceive ourselves and the truth is not in us. [9]If

we confess our sins, he is faithful and just and will forgive us our sins and purify us from all unrighteousness.

The best time to step back into proper habits is right after you realize you have stepped out! Our journey with food, like our walk with God, is one where we must constantly rely on God's strength to uphold us in times of weakness. Remember what Jesus said in Mark 10:27, "With man this is impossible, but not with God; all things are possible with God."

DISCOVERY QUESTIONS

1. How are you feeling about your food journey as we near the end of this discovery series? Do you feel encouraged or fearful about your future journey? If you are fearful, what measures could you put in place to keep you going after the study ends?

2. Have you discovered any new mind hacks that help you feel more satisfied with reasonable portions?

3. Rate how you are dealing with entertainment eating (great) 10 - 1 (not in control). What habits do you need to develop (e.g., decide what you will eat beforehand, eat a healthy snack before you go, always eat a salad first with dressing on the side)?

Prayer Time

The process can seem intimidating, but we have our secret weapon in Jesus. He can supply strength and new perspective where and when we lack it.

Hebrews 12:1-3

[1]Therefore, since we are surrounded by such a great cloud of witnesses, let us throw off everything that hinders and the sin that so easily entangles, and let us run with perseverance the race marked out for us. [2]Let us fix our eyes on Jesus, the author and perfecter of our faith, who for the joy set before him endured the cross, scorning its shame, and sat down at the right

hand of the throne of God. [3]Consider him who endured such opposition from sinful men, so that you will not grow weary and lose heart.

Make this your daily prayer:

God give me strength to throw off everything that hinders; to run with perseverance and to fix my eyes on Jesus. May I always consider Him who endured opposition and may that revelation give me the extra push I need to not grow weary or lose heart. Amen.

On Your Own

You need to keep in mind that...

Hebrews 12:11-13

[11]No discipline seems pleasant at the time, but painful. Later on, however, it produces a harvest of righteousness and peace for those who have been trained by it. [12]Therefore, strengthen your feeble arms and weak knees. [13]"Make level paths for your feet," so that the lame may not be disabled, but rather healed.

Initially, habit formation is anything but automatic. In fact, it can even feel restrictive. But, as with many of life skills, the more you practice, the better you get. The eventual goal of successful habit formation is to get to the point where you automatically perform an action without conscious thought.

Hebrews 12:12-13a reminds us that strengthening our feeble arms and weak knees will keep us from wobbling or veering from the path. Good form is essential for a runner to finish well. Also, the discipline of healthy habits levels out the path and keeps us from tripping up along the way.

This week, you were asked to decide on new go-to habits to put in place of each of your old habits.

Let's look at *Find Your Weigh* p. 144-145 (desserts) and p. 147 (general habits) for some examples of workable habits.

(Take note: All of us are different, so it's not possible to come up with a one-size-fits-all to meet everyone's needs. Some of these examples may work perfectly for you, but you may need to come up with different habits to address your particular needs.)

Write down any habits you intend to implement.

_____

_____

_____

CLOSING SESSION

Walk in the Truth

This study was created to lead you on a journey of discovery, to uncover what motivates and informs your decisions about food... to reveal the truth.

> John 8:31-32
>
> [31]To the Jews who had believed him, Jesus said, "If you hold to my teaching, you are really my disciples. [32]Then you will know the truth, and the truth will set you free."

How did the disciples finally come to accept Jesus as the Truth? They walked with Him, they talked with Him and they spent time with Him.

In verse 31, what is the evidence that they are His disciples?

_____

_____

_____

In essence, you have been doing the same thing as the disciples for the last seven weeks. You started on this journey knowing only one thing...you had a problem with food and you wanted to fix it. Since then, you have spent time exploring your thoughts and mindset about food, exploring God's Word for insights and spending time with others who are walking the very same road as you.

Hopefully, God's truth has penetrated your thinking and will illuminate your path from now on.

Yet, we know that knowledge itself is not enough to keep us from straying. If Jesus is the Truth and the disciples are your examples, what must you do to stay on track from this day forward?

_____

_____

_____

Video

> *Refer to the following outline as you watch the video. Make note of anything that stands out to you for further reflection or discussion.*

- God's promises

- How you leave this place today is up to you

Video Discussion and Bible Study

- The promises are there...but the follow-through is still in your hands.

- Read 2 Corinthians 1:20-21.

   [20]For no matter how many promises God has made, they are "Yes" in Christ. And so through him the "Amen" is spoken by us to the glory of God. [21]Now it is God who makes both us and you

stand firm in Christ. He anointed us, [22]set his seal of ownership on us, and put His Spirit in our hearts as a deposit, guaranteeing what is to come.

You have all God's promises at our disposal, but how are you going to say "Amen" to those promises as this study comes to an end?

◆ The biggest obstacle to continued success with our weight is that we fail to get back up and keep going after we fall. Perfection is not the point...we need Jesus. Read 2 Corinthians 1:21 one more time...how must our Amen be spoken?

◆ We have learned a lot about God's promises over the last weeks.

> We are blessed when we listen to what God reveals.
>
> We have the resident power of the Holy Spirit, the same Spirit that raised Christ from the dead, living in us.
>
> We don't have to set our minds on earthly things because our lives are hidden with Christ.
>
> No law or set of rules is a match for the Holy Spirit's work in our lives.
>
> We can approach God boldly with our struggles. Our advocate Jesus understands and sympathizes with our struggles.
>
> We can stand firm on our freedom in Christ.
>
> Establishing new habits may be painful in the beginning, but they can bring peace.

Talk about some habits you intend to implement to say "Amen" to these promises in a practical way from this day forward.

> *If we consciously knew what made us click with food, if we understand exactly what propels us and causes us to feel so helpless to its draw, then we would do something about it!*
>
> **FYW, p. 17**

If there's one thing that our past struggles have taught us, it's that we will never be perfect in regard to our food choices. In fact, this realization can and will keep us grounded as we walk out our new reality and act on the truth after this study ends.

Philippians 3:12-14

[12]Not that I have already obtained all this, or have already been made perfect, but I press on to take hold of that for which Christ Jesus took hold of me. [13]Brothers, I do not consider myself yet to have taken hold of it. But one thing I do: Forgetting what is behind and straining toward what is ahead, [14]I press on toward the goal to win the prize for which God has called me heavenward in Christ Jesus.

Paul acknowledged that he did not have all the answers, but he refused to give up even when faced with the glaring reality of his continued weakness. In fact, he reinforced his determination to keep going and to press on.

In verse 12, Paul wrote, "I press on to take hold of that for which Christ Jesus took hold of me."

What is it we are pressing on to take hold of? Christ extended and continues to extend His grace in times of need. So, He welcomes us to press on and take hold of (to rely on and to seek) His grace each and every time we struggle.

Are you prepared to approach Jesus honestly and openly and ask for His grace when you face new struggles and temptations on your weight journey? _____

If so, you have reached an important goal of this study!

◆ Learn to bring my struggles with food to God and lay them bare before Him on a regular basis.

Again, in verse 14, Paul asserted, "I press on _____ _____ _____ _____ _____ _____ _____for which God has called me heavenward in Christ Jesus."

Paul knew that his ultimate prize would come only when he went to heaven, still he resolved to continually forget the past and to strain toward what was ahead for the rest of his life. Despite the fact that he still did not consider himself to have taken hold of or mastered his weaknesses, he did not use those weaknesses as an excuse to give up.

When will we finish our weight journey? Likely, our need to consider our food choices will not stop short of heaven. But then, we have an eternity of no food worries to look forward to...we all can say amen to that!

Are you in it for the long haul, understanding that you will likely have to walk this road and navigate some potholes along the way?

If you answered yes to this, then you have internalized another two important goals of this study!

- See healthy weight management as a journey, rather than a destination.

- Replace the diet mentality with a long-term mindset.

DISCOVERY QUESTIONS

1. What is the greatest truth you will take away from this study?

2. Last week, you were asked to determine a new put-on habit for each old habit you wanted to replace. What is one of your new habits?

3. What aspect of God do you now understand and appreciate more clearly since starting this study?

FINAL GOALS REVIEW

Read through each of the study goals. Write your initials by each goal you now recognize as truth and intend to implement from this day forward.

_____See healthy weight management as a journey, rather than a destination.

_____Regard healthy weight management in terms of daily choices, rather as an "all or nothing" proposition.

_____Replace the diet mentality with a long-term mindset.

_____Become more mindful during every step of the eating process (choices, prep, actually sitting down to eat).

_____Learn to bring my struggles with food to God and lay them bare before Him on a regular basis.

_____Develop a healthy perspective about my weight by accepting the body I have today.

_____Understand and acknowledge that my worth and value as a child of God is not found in my weight or appearance.

Prayer Time

It has to be a step-by-step journey. Small daily decisions and behavior changes can make a difference for the long haul.

If you've had a setbacks, pick yourself up and keep going.

If you have plateaued well short of your ultimate goal, keep going.

If you've lost the majority of your weight, it can be extremely unnerving and scary to know what to do next, keep going.

The longer you persevere, the more confident you will become. The more confident you become, the more natural your new habits will seem.

The more natural your eating habits seem, the less you think about them. The less you have to think about your eating habits, the more they become a part of you.

The more they become a part of you, the less you remember your old journey. The less you remember your old journey, the more you can embrace your new one; keep going!

FYW, p. 160-161

Finally, let's pray the following Scripture as a prayer for each other.

Ephesians 1:17-23

[17]I keep asking that the God of our Lord Jesus Christ, the glorious Father, may give you the Spirit of wisdom and revelation, so that you may know him better. [18]I pray also that the eyes of your heart may be enlightened in order that you may know the hope to

which he has called you, the riches of his glorious inheritance in the saints, [19]and his incomparably great power for us who believe. That power is like the working of his mighty strength, [20]which he exerted in Christ when he raised him from the dead and seated him at his right hand in the heavenly realms, [21]far above all rule and authority, power and dominion, and every title that can be given, not only the present age but also in the one to come. [22]And God placed all things under his feet and appointed him to be head over everything for the church, [23]which is his body, the fullness of who fills everything in every way. Amen.

Printed in Great Britain
by Amazon

42194892R00059